LETTER TRACING

B is for....

D is for....

Ball

Doll

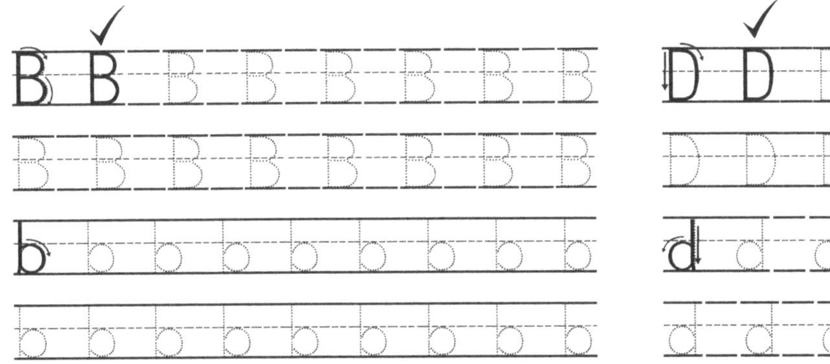

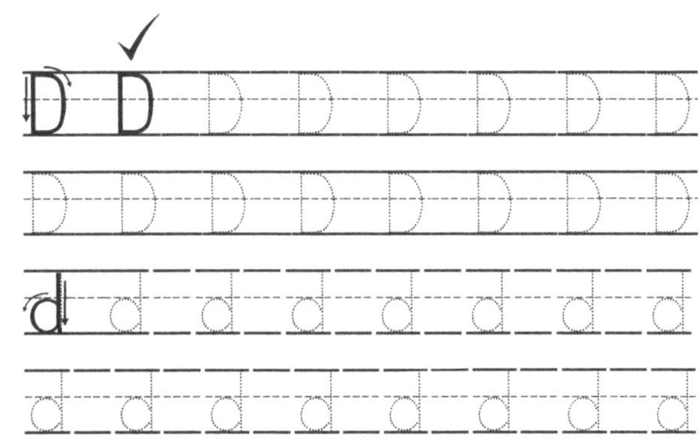

**Follow the gray dots
to form the letters**

B is for....

Bag

B B B B B B B B B

B B B B B B B B B

B B B B B B B B B

B B B B B B B B B

B B B B b b b b

b b b b b b b b b

b b b b b b b b b

b b b b b b b b b

b b b b b b b b b

C is for....

Cat

D is for....

Duck

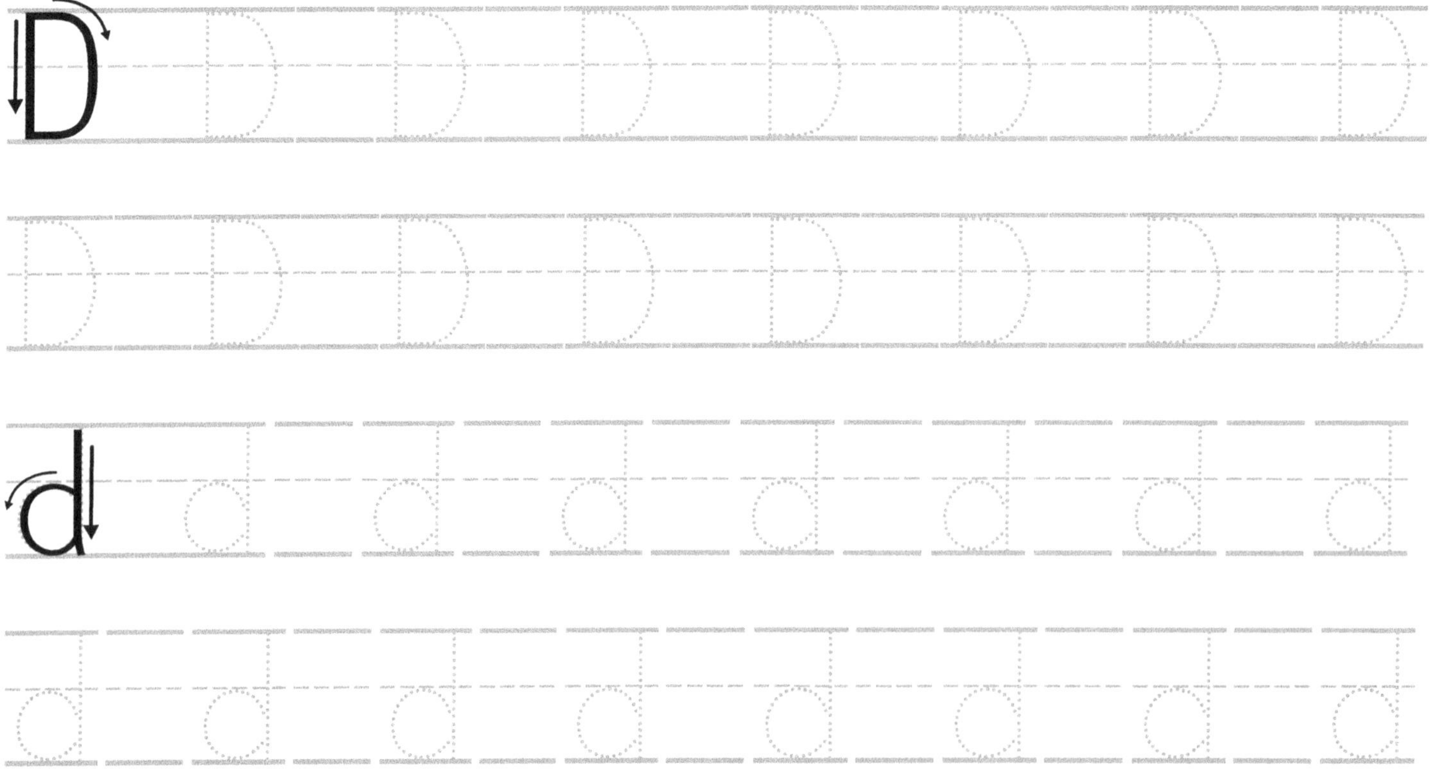

E is for....

Elephant

F is for....

Flamingo

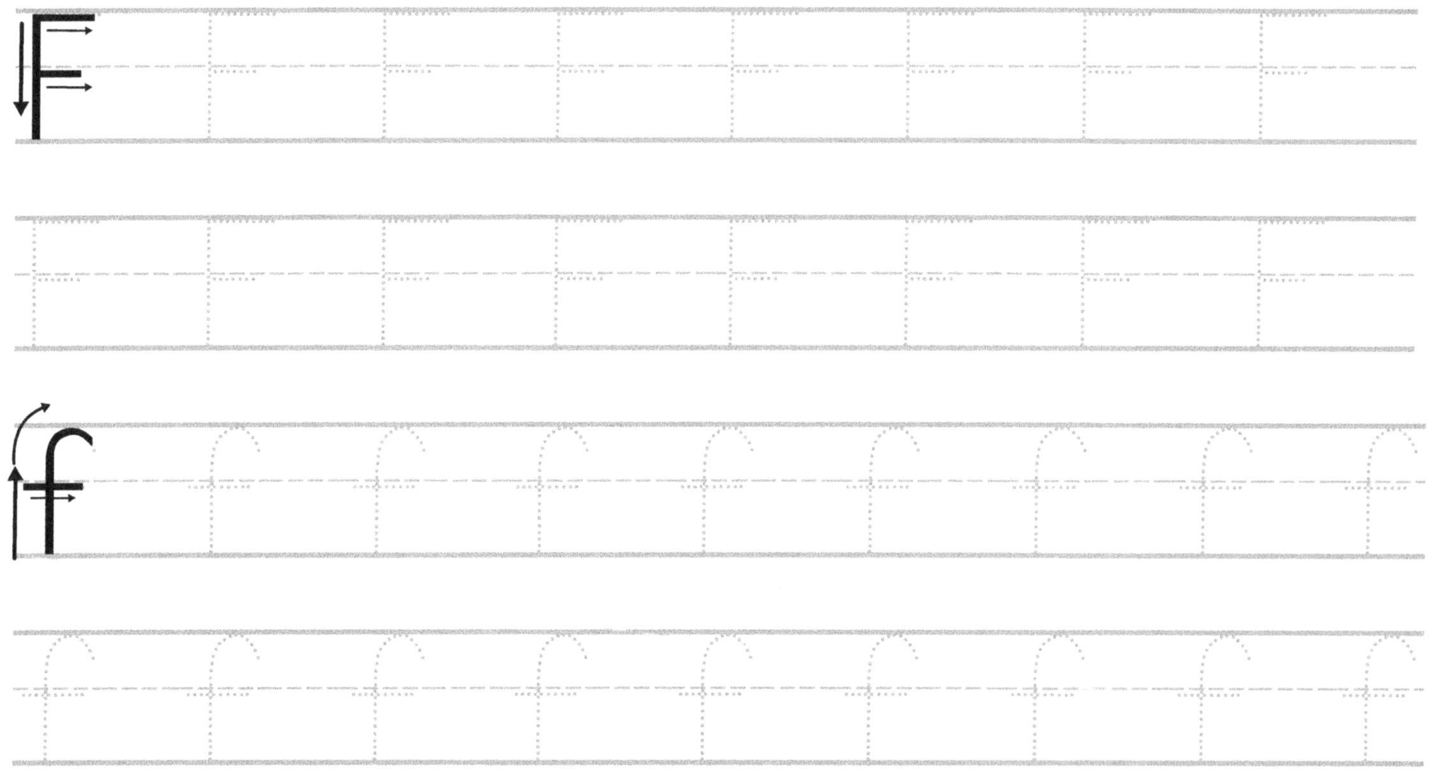

G is for....

Goose

H is for....

Home

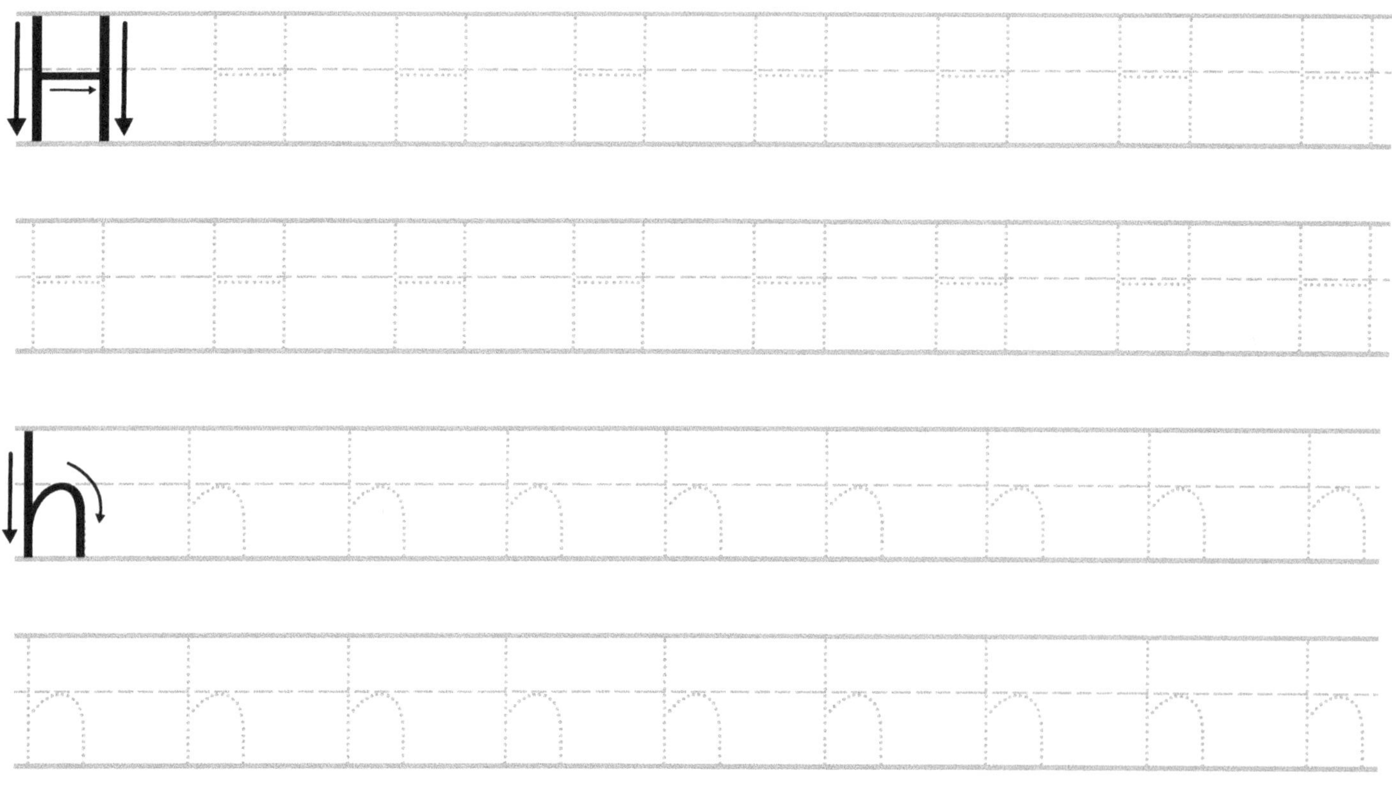

I is for....

Ice cream

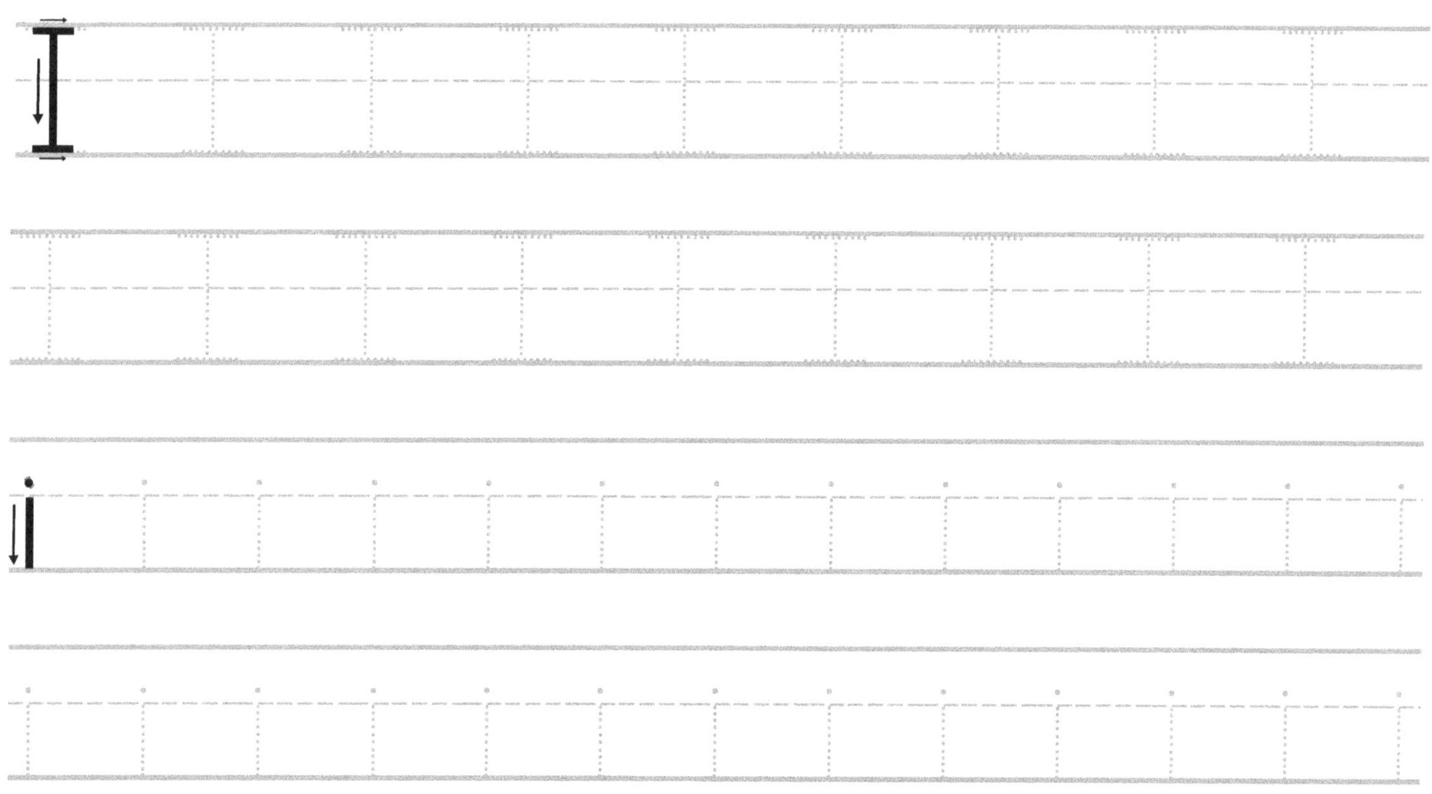

J is for....

Jellyfish

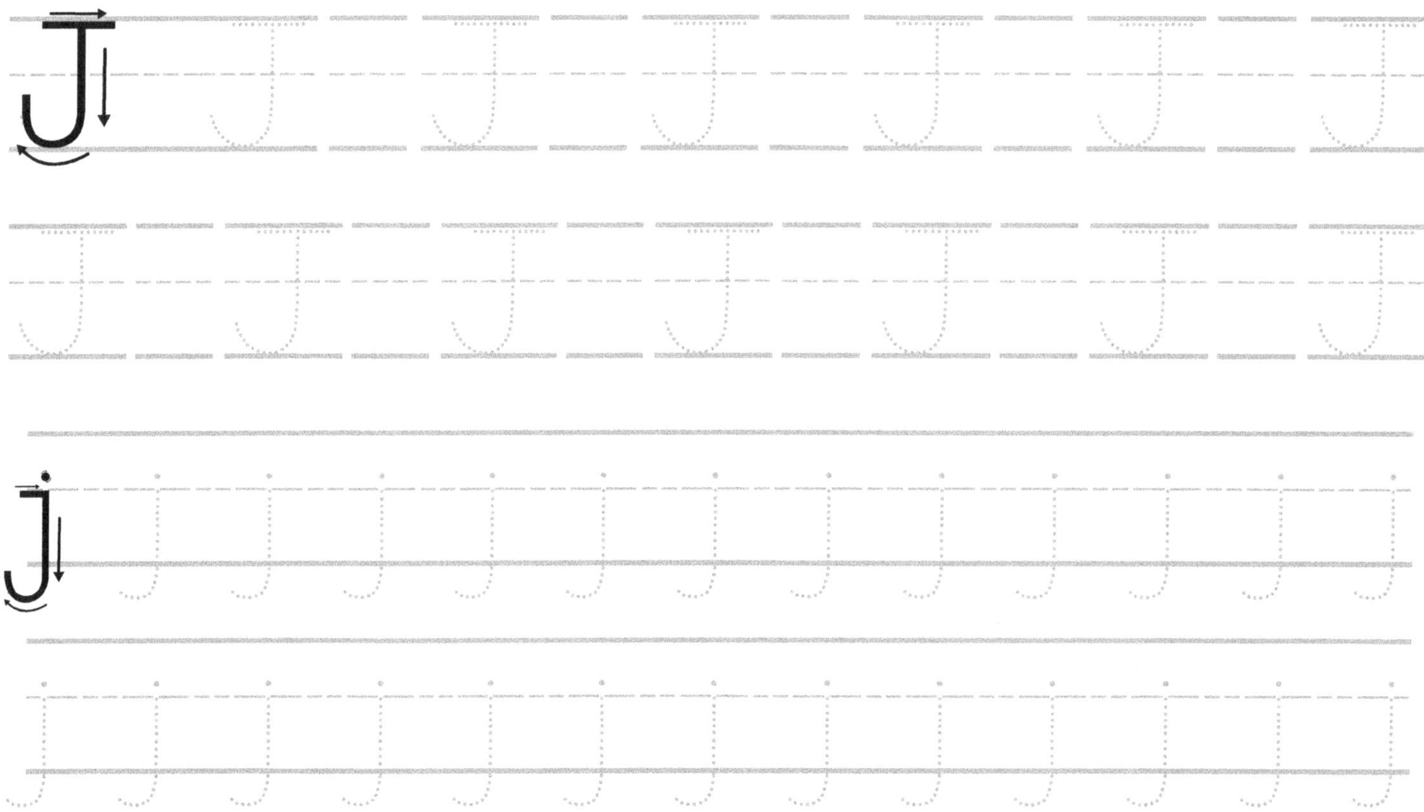

K is for....

Kangaroo

L is for....

Lamp

M is for....

Milk

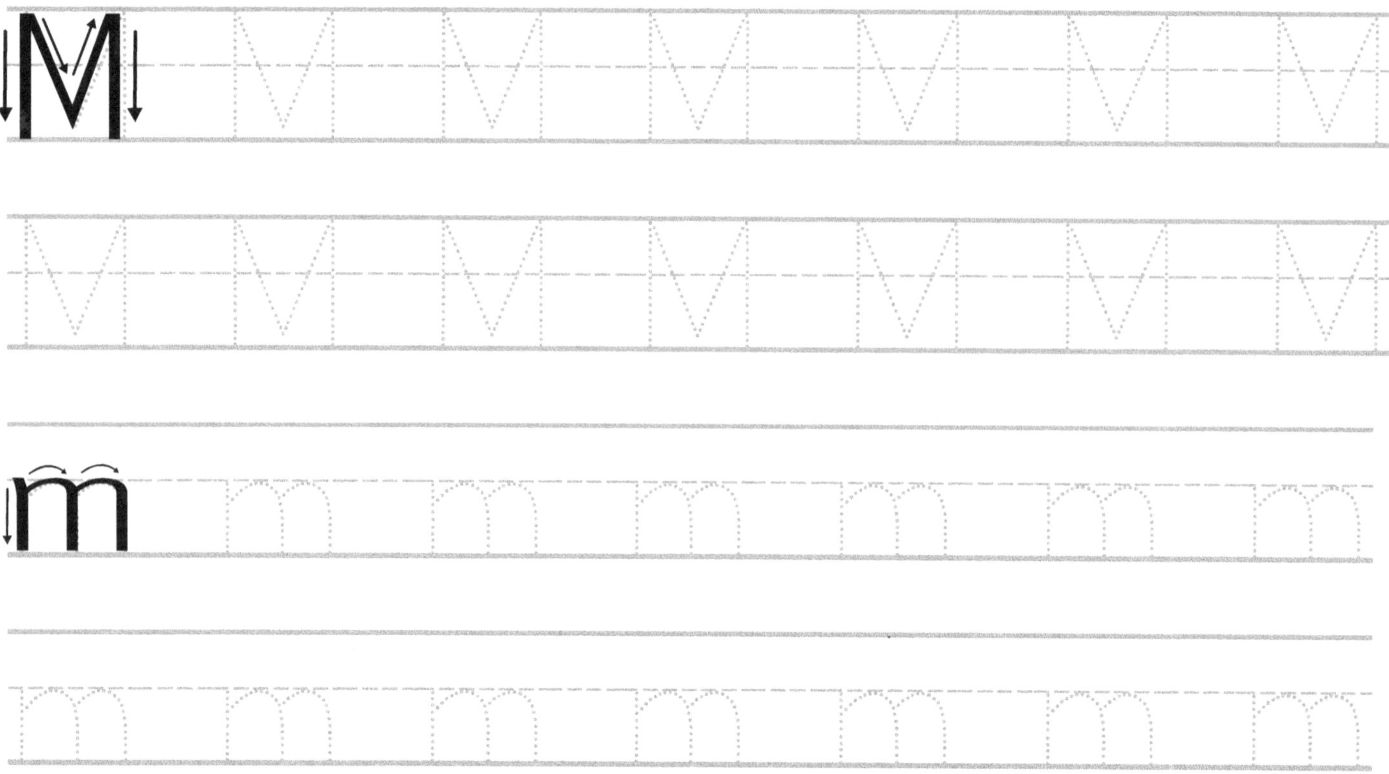

N is for....

Ninja

O is for....

Owl

P is for....

Panda

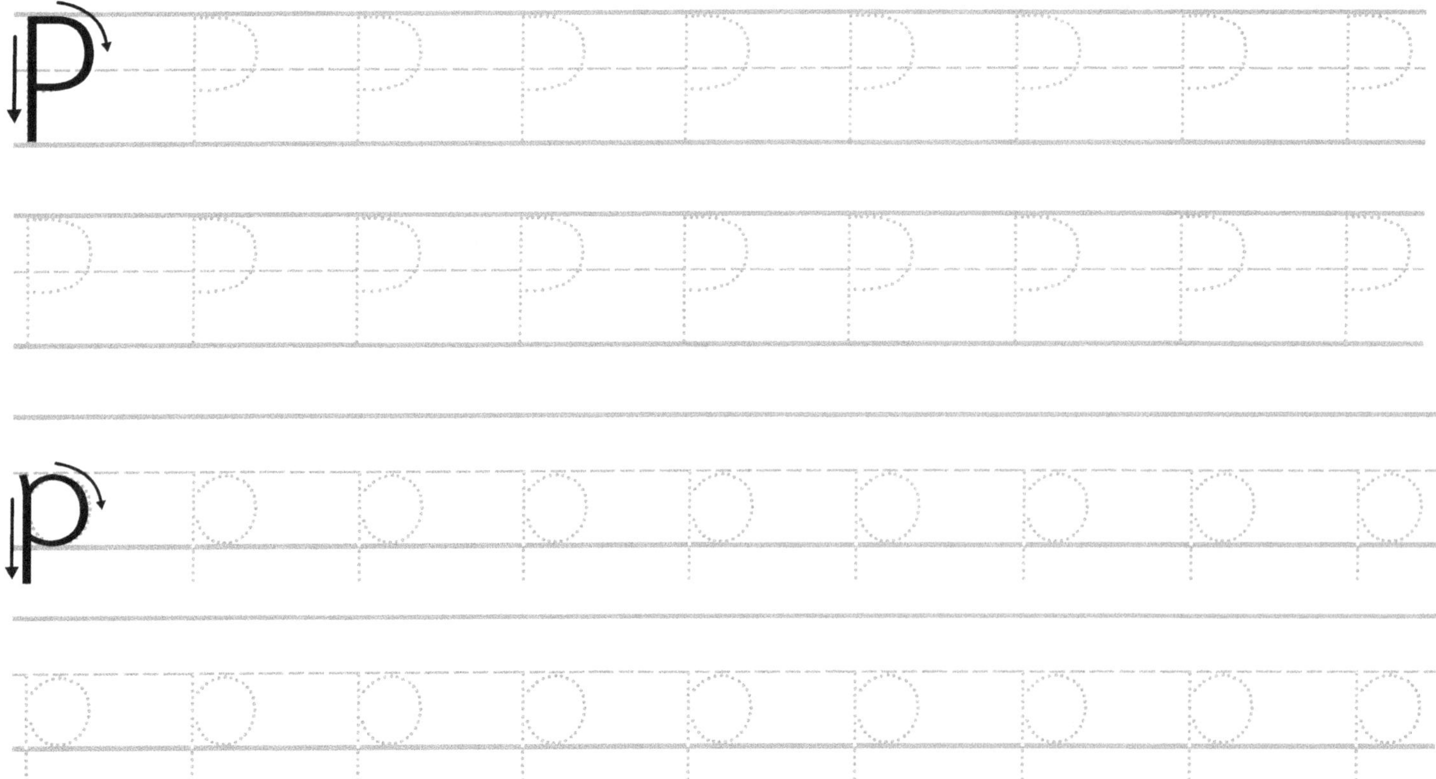

p p p p p p p p p

p p p p p p p p p

p p p p p p p p p

p p p p p p p p p

p p p p p p p p p

p p p p p p p p p

p p p p p p p p p

p p p p p p p p p

p p p p p p p p p

Q is for....

Quill

R is for....

Robot

S is for....

Star

T is for....

Turtle

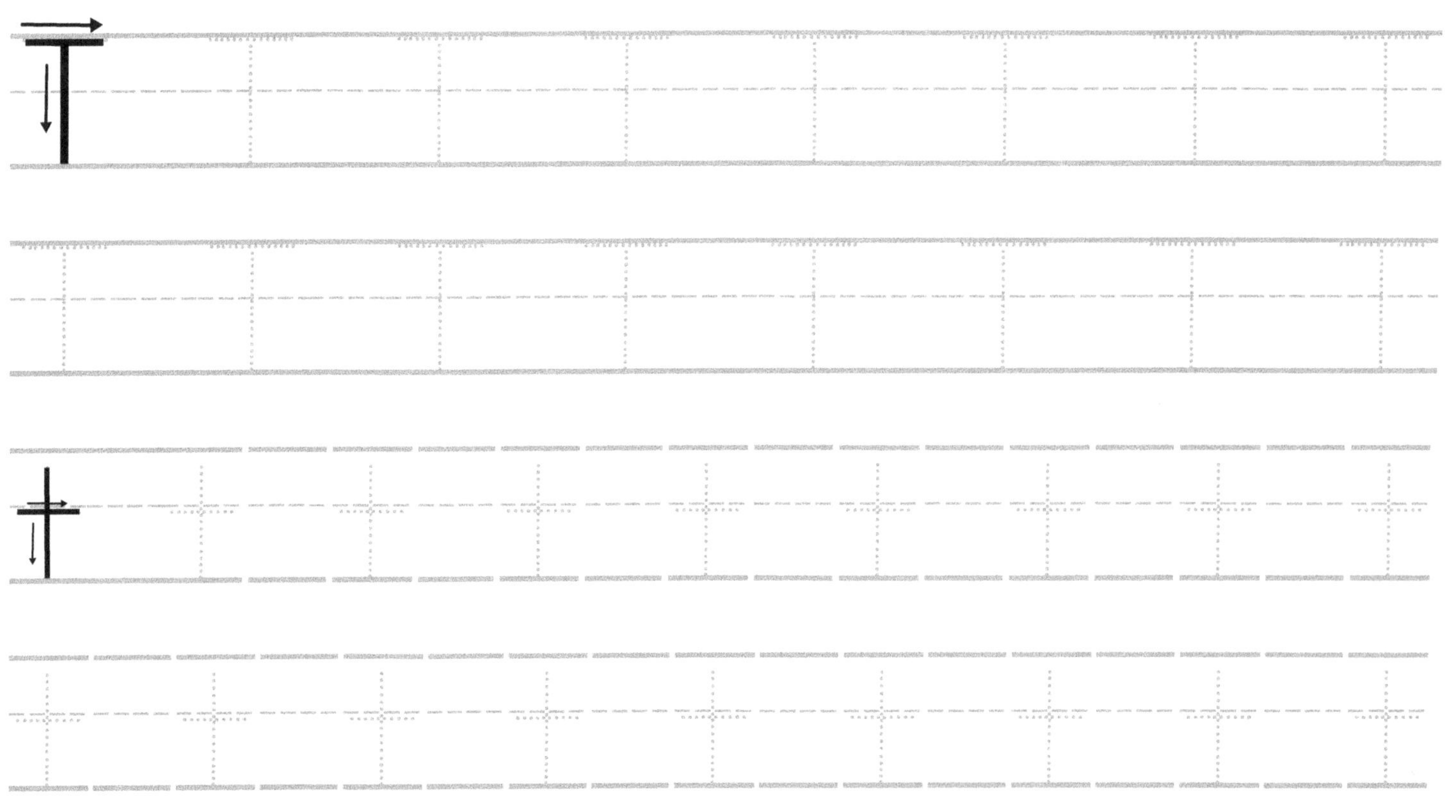

U is for....

Umbrella

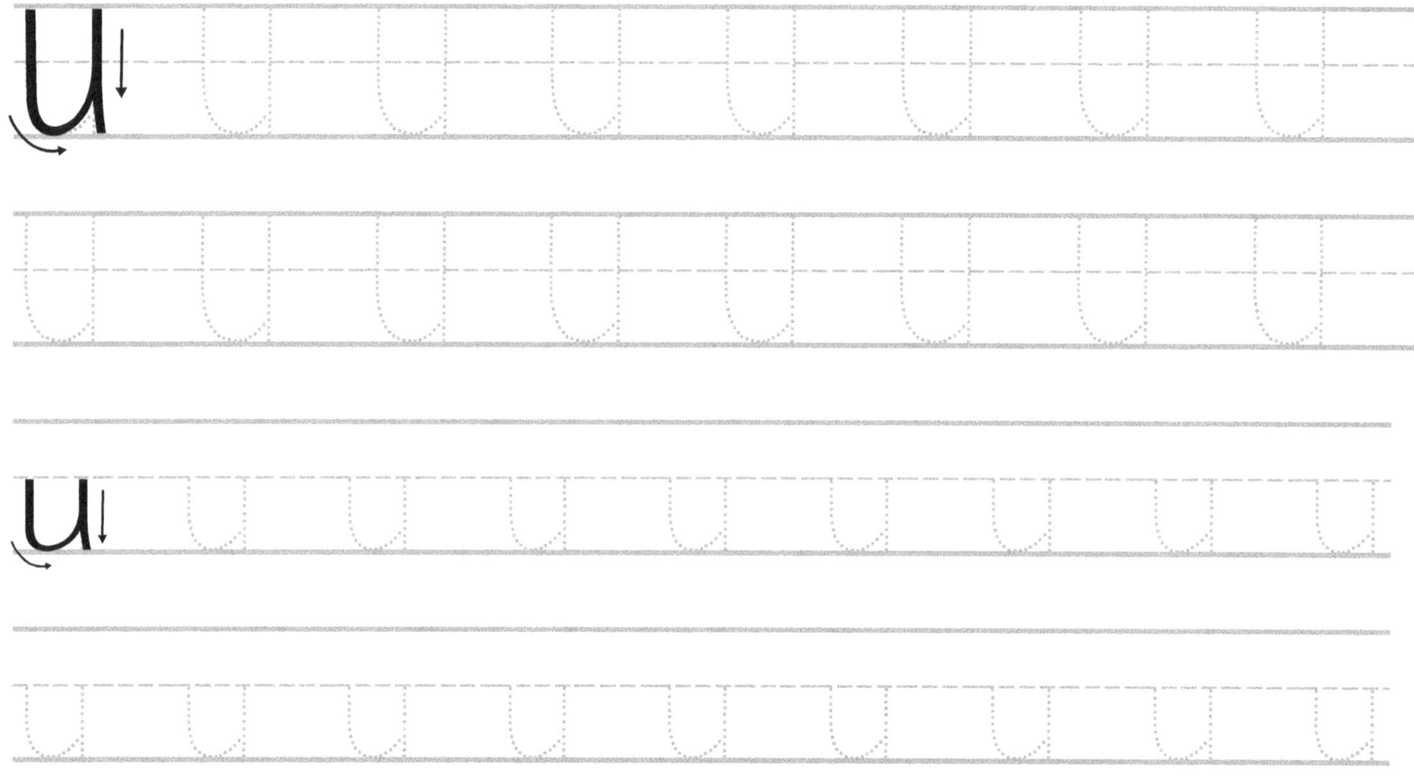

V is for....

Vehicle

W is for....

Wolf

X is for....

X-ray

Y is for....

Yo Yo

Z is for....

Zebra

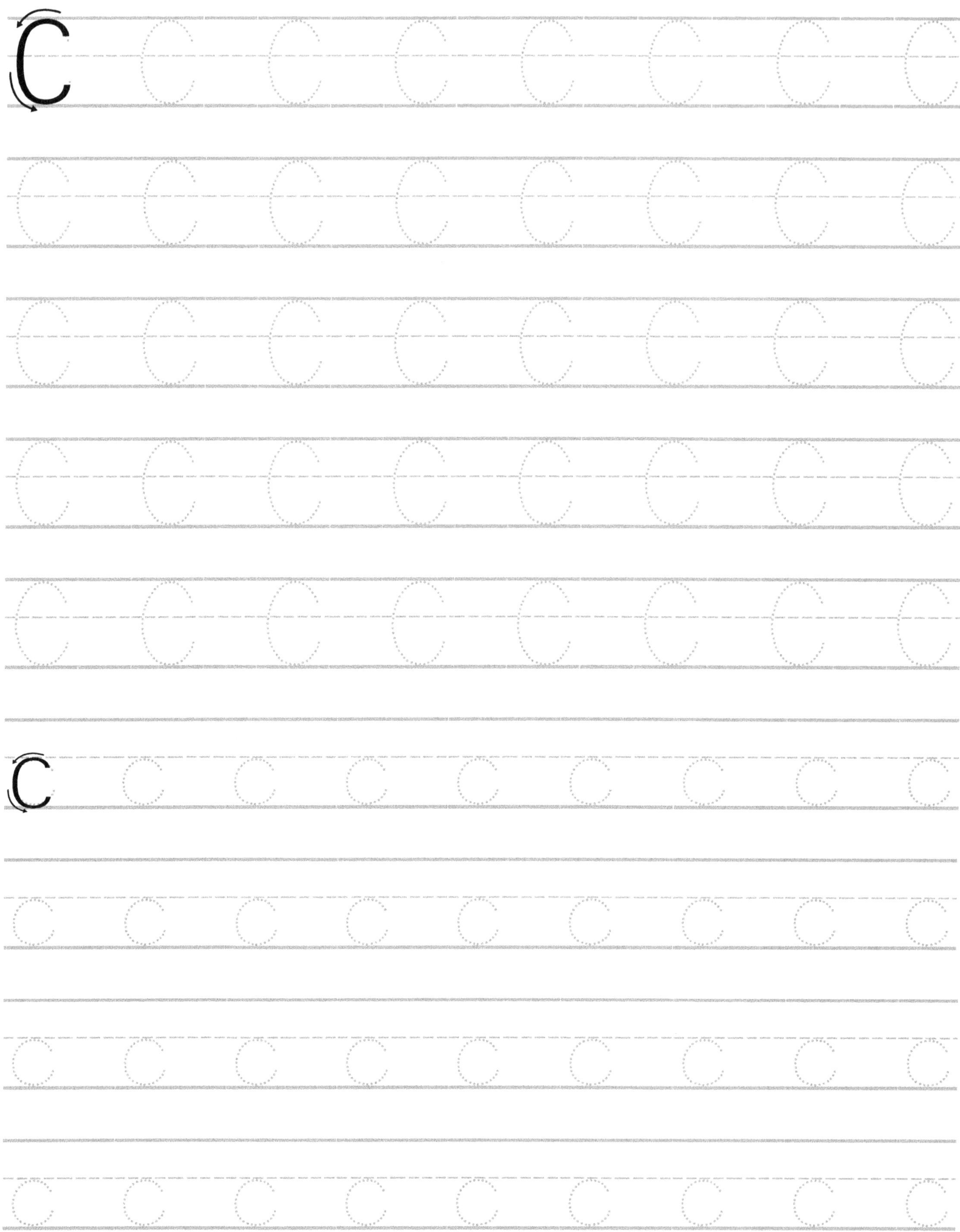

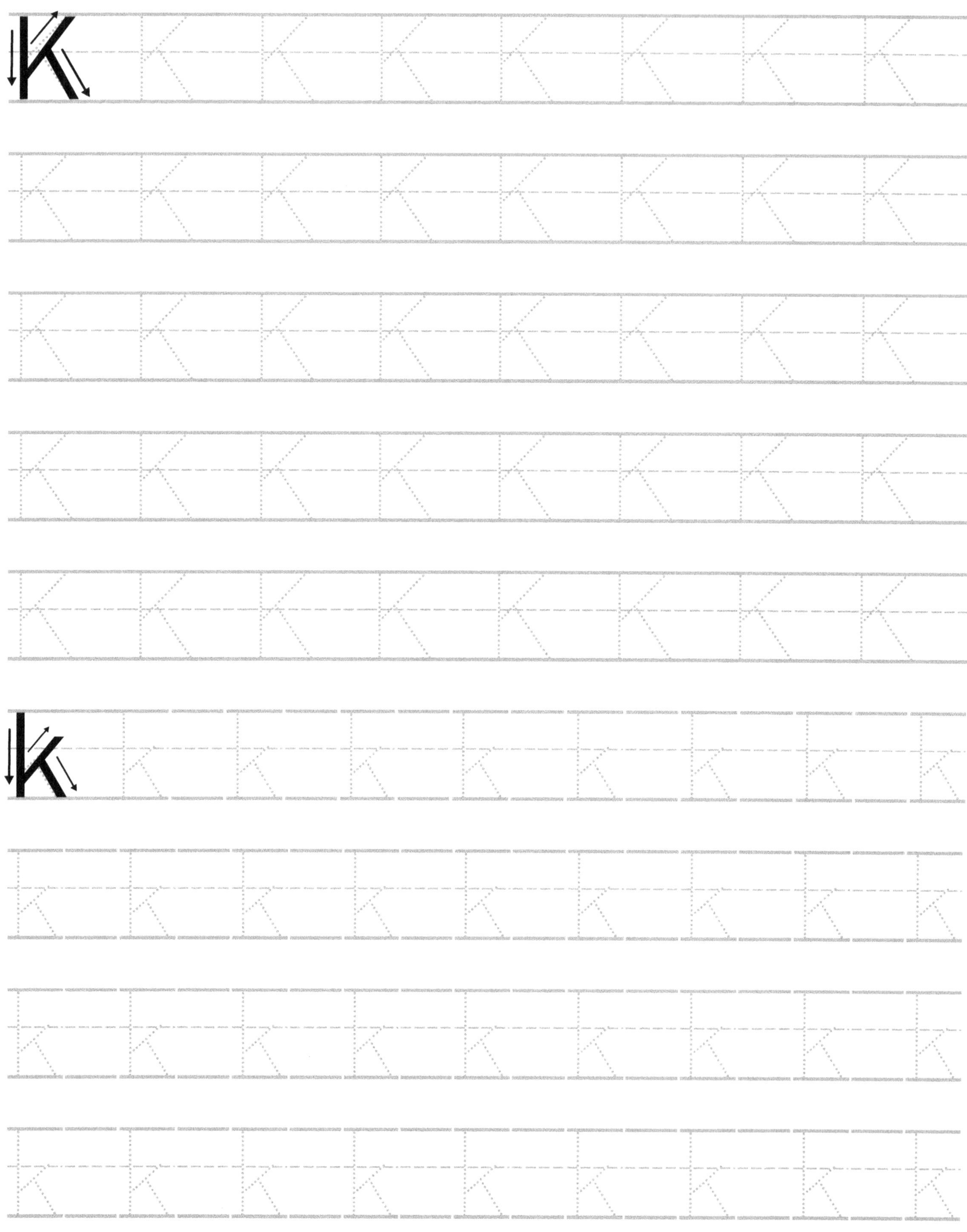

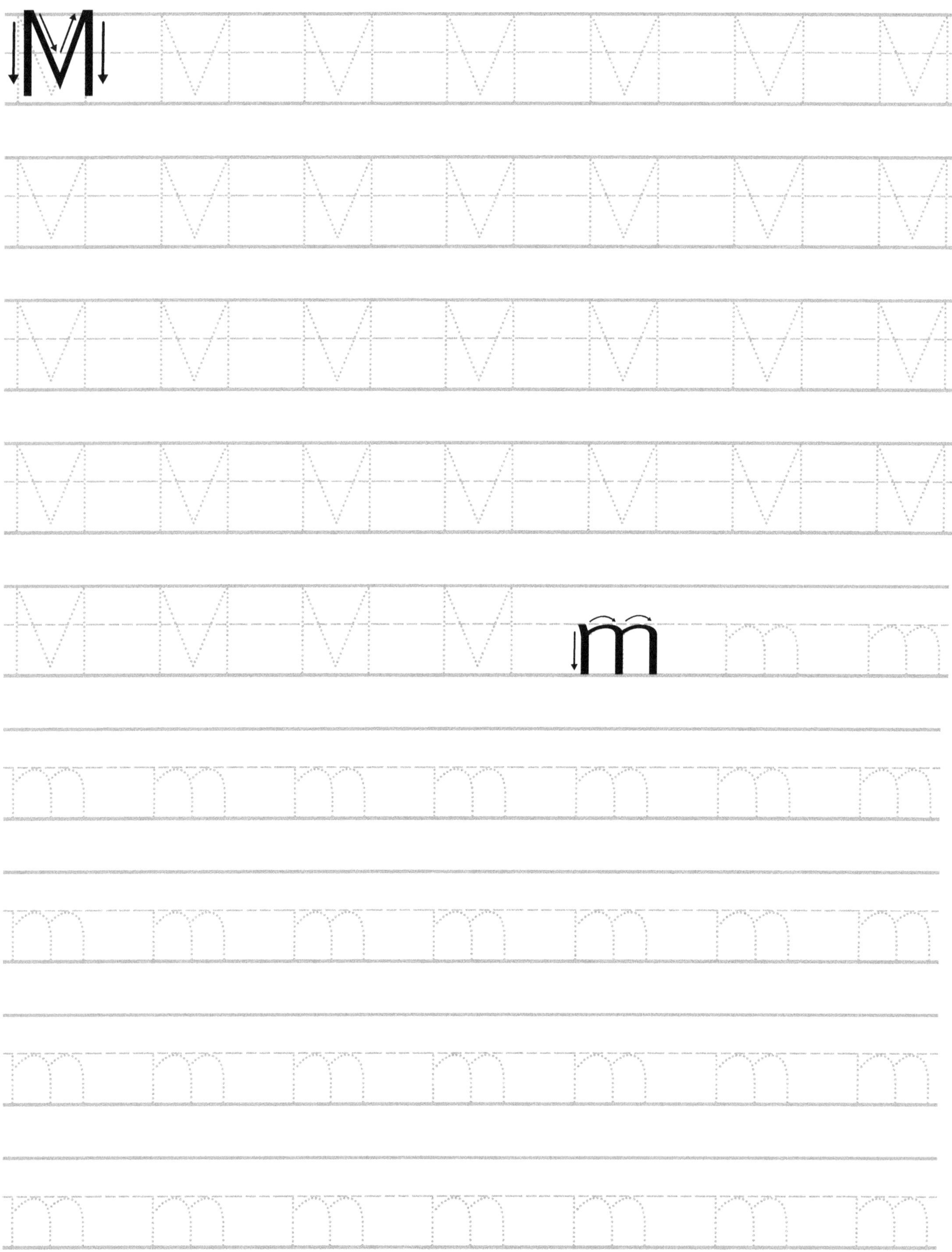

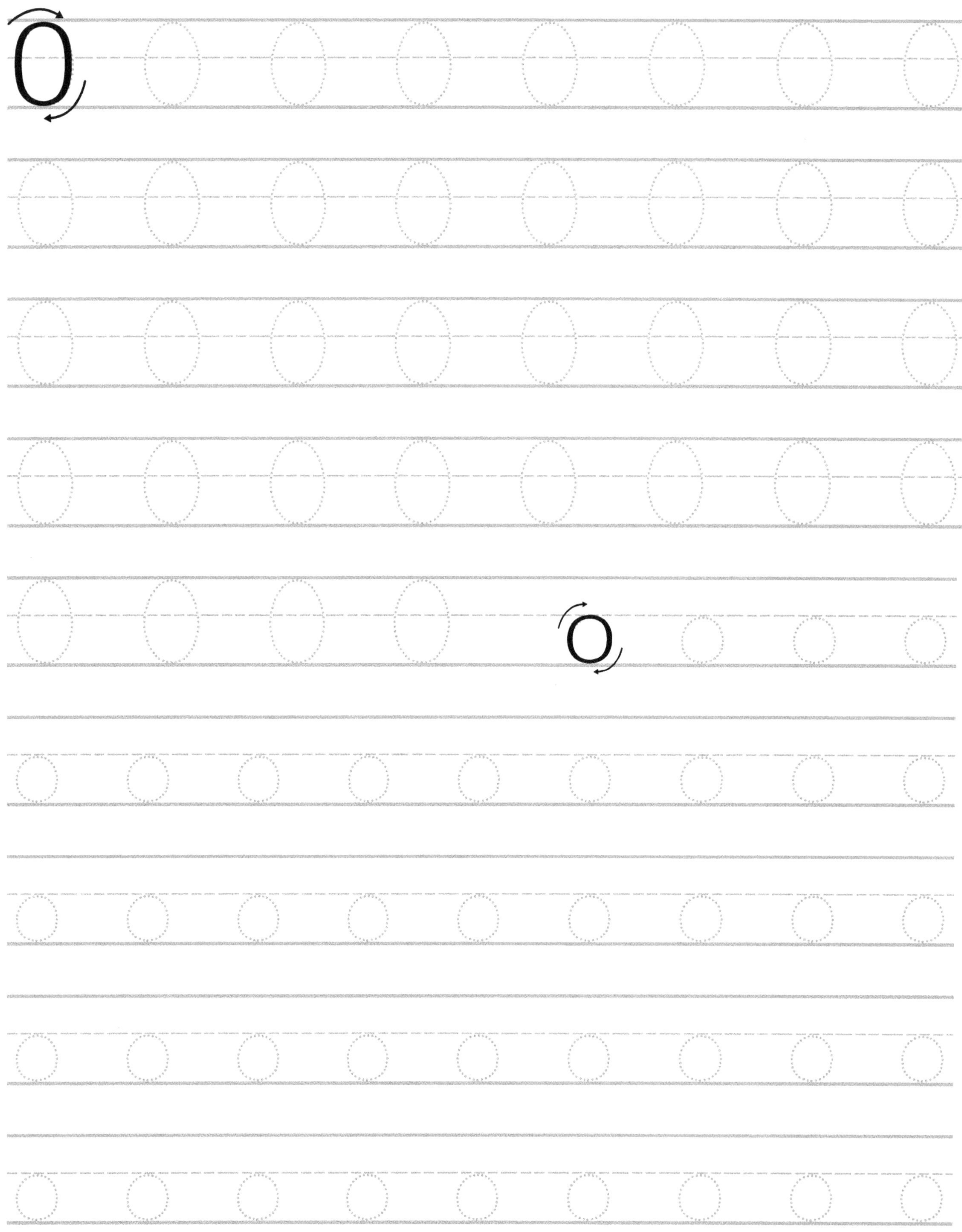

P

p

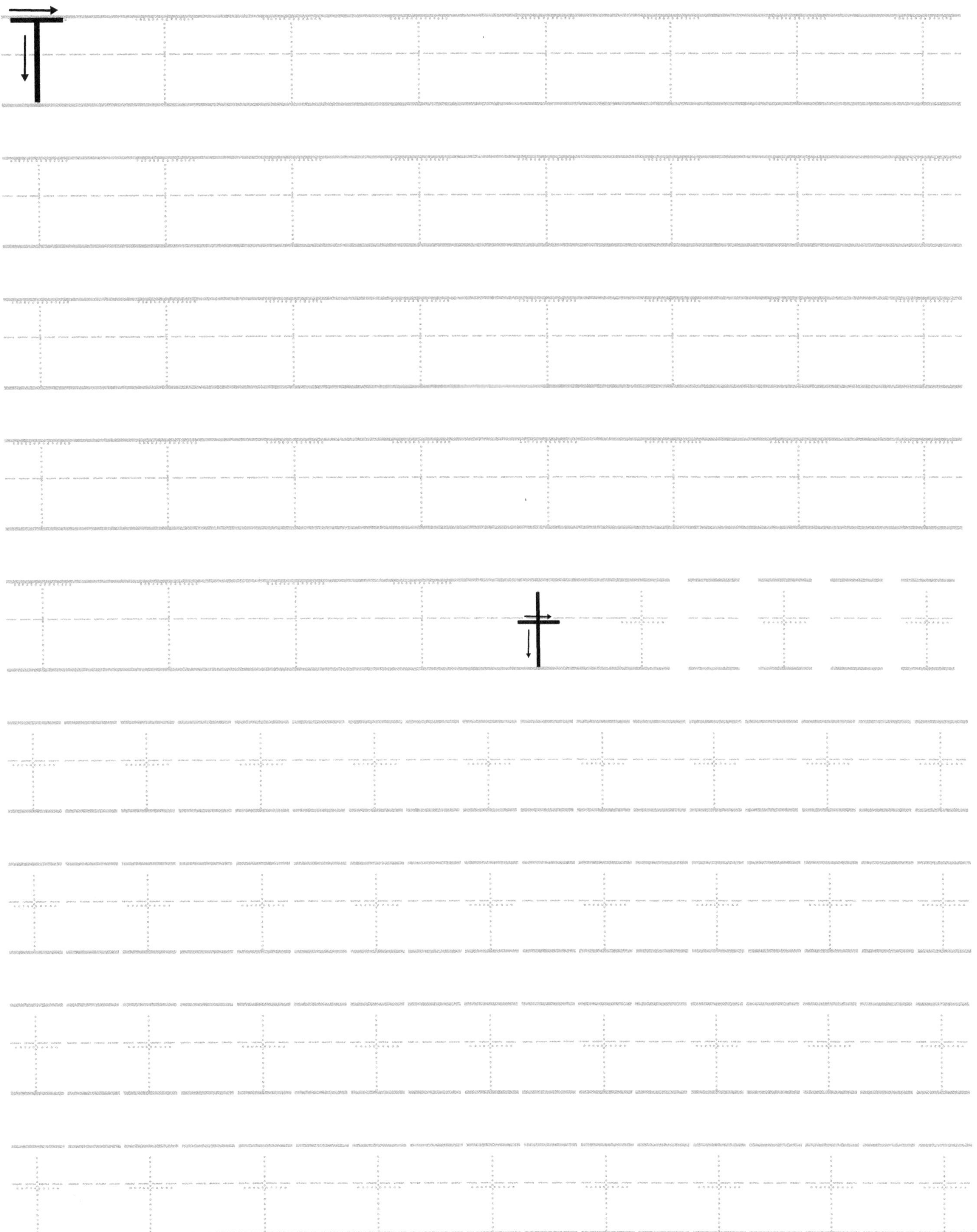

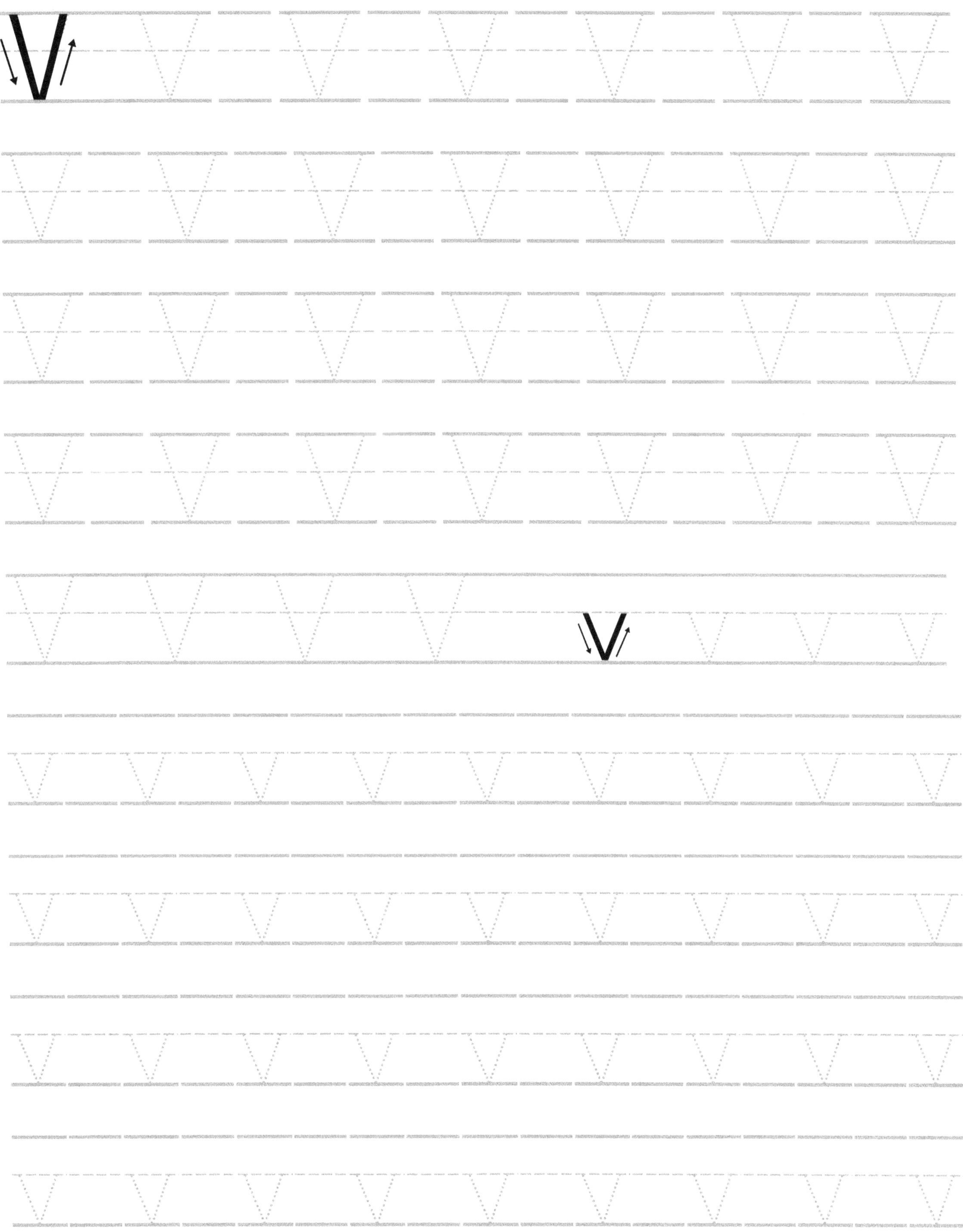